I0843465

THANKSGIVING
COLORING BOOK
FOR KIDS

SIMPLE BIG PICTURES HAPPY HOLIDAY COLORING BOOKS FOR TODDLERS AND PRESCHOOLERS

The Coloring Book Art Design Studio

THANKSGIVING
COLORING BOOK FOR KIDS

by The Coloring Book Art Design Studio

THANKSGIVING
COLORING BOOK FOR KIDS

Copyright © 2018 by The Coloring Book Art Design Studio

All rights reserved. No part of this publication may be reproduced, distributed, or transmitted in any form or by any means, including photocopying, recording, or other electronic or mechanical methods, without the prior written permission of the publisher, except in the case of brief quotations embodied in critical reviews and certain other noncommercial uses permitted by copyright law.

THIS BOOK

BELONG TO

____

____

LET'S TEST YOUR COLOR

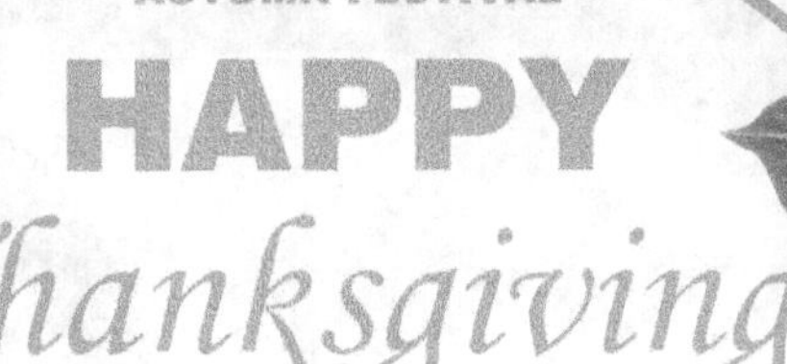

AUTUMN FESTIVAL
HAPPY
Thanksgiving

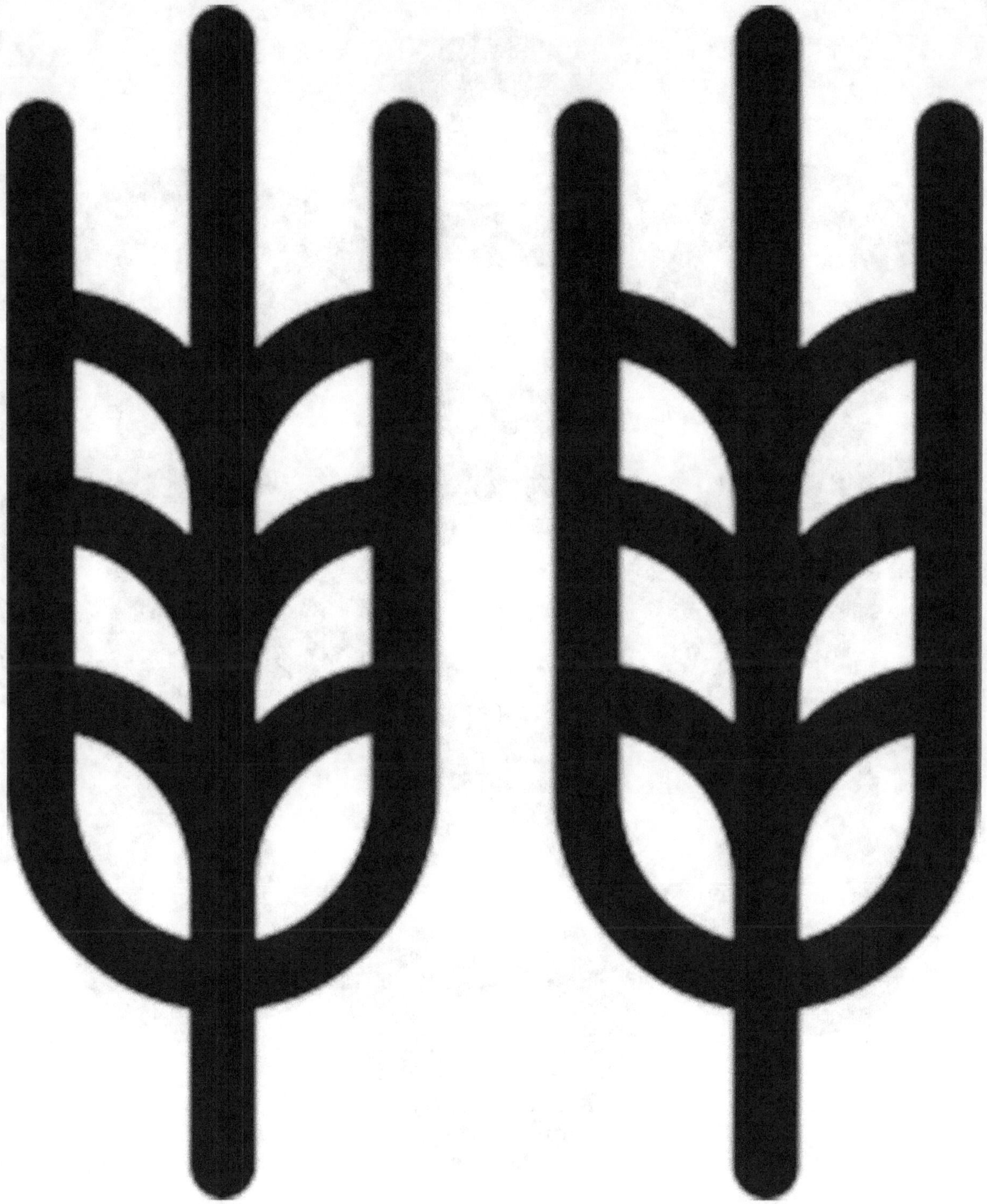

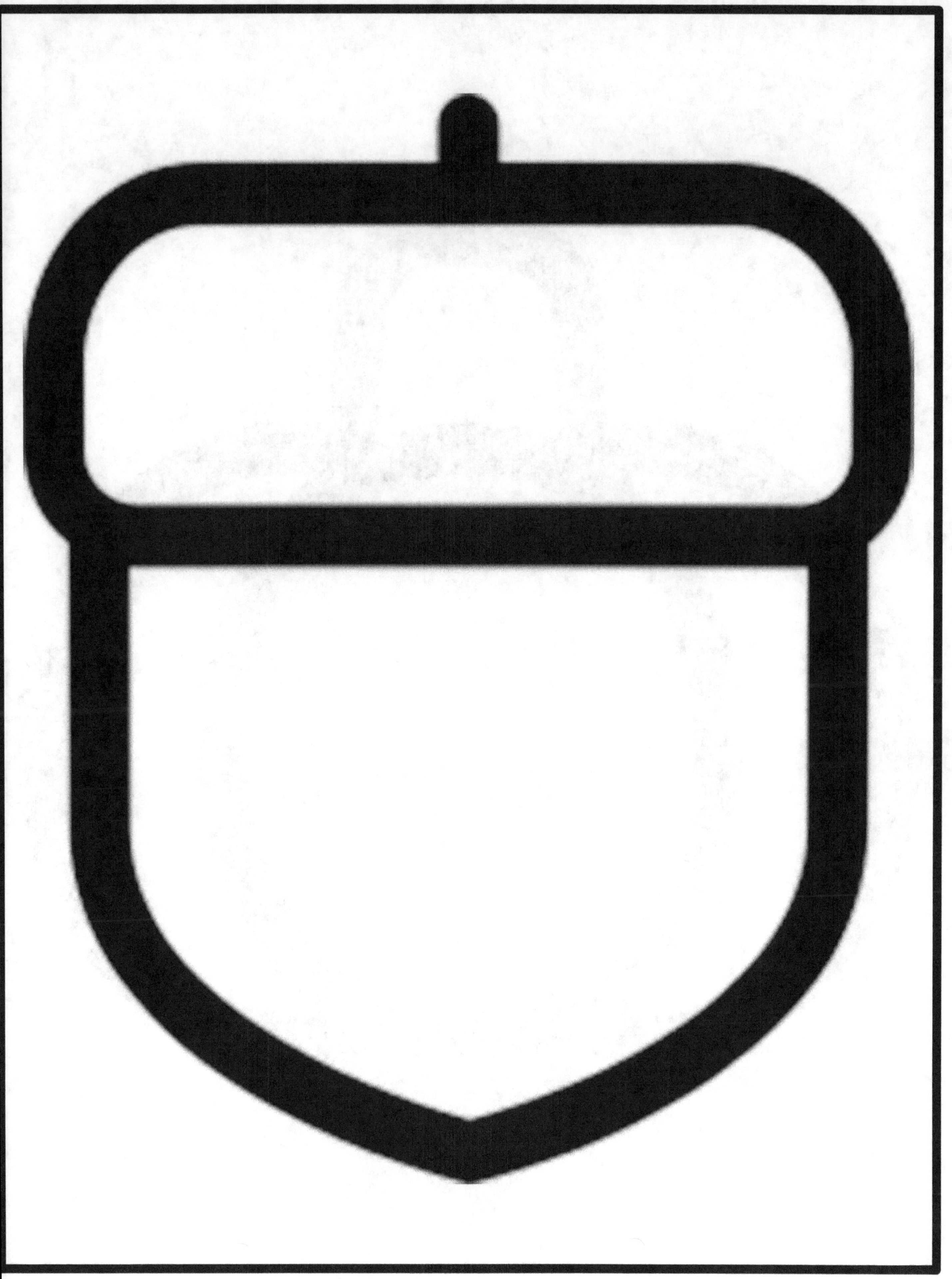

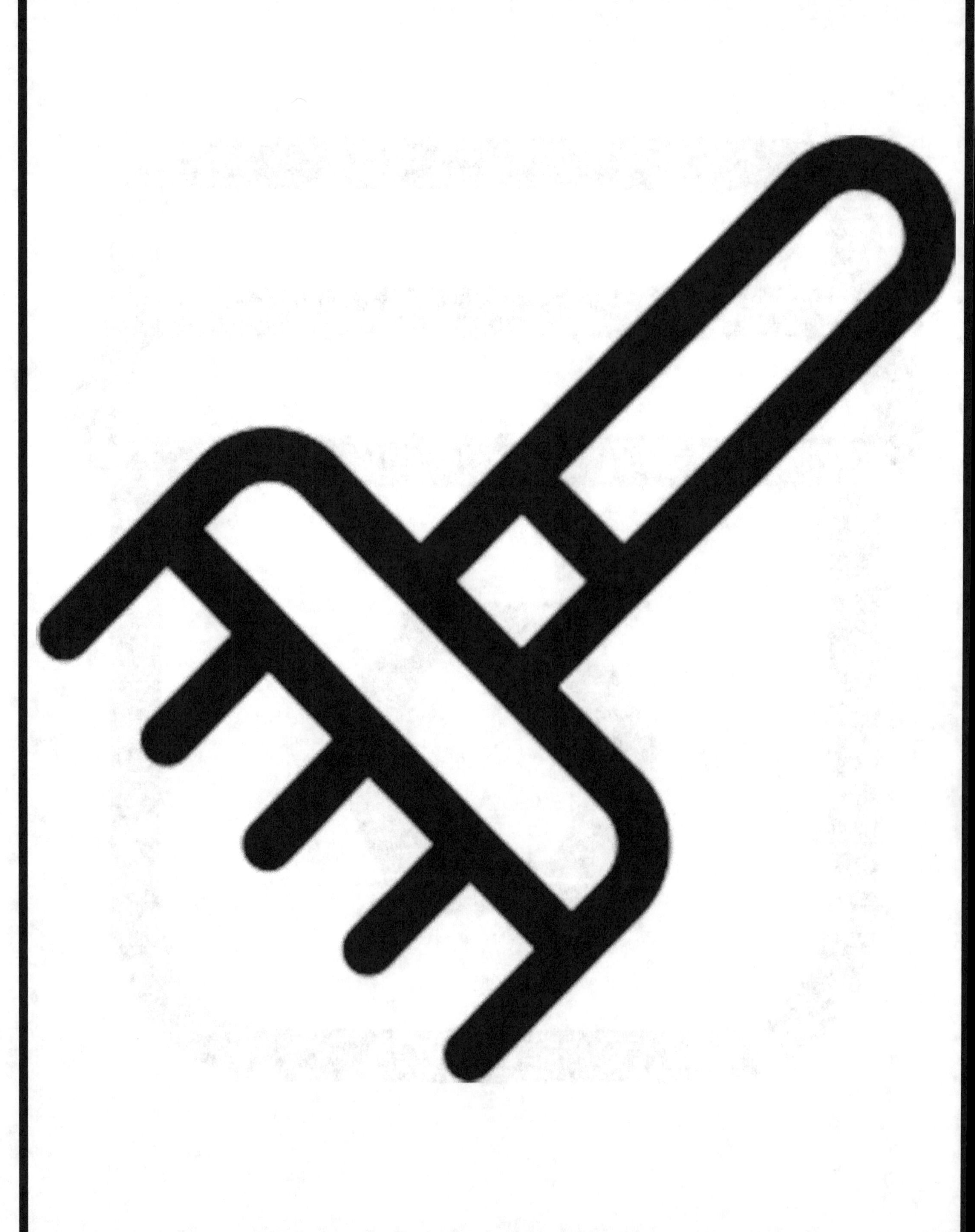

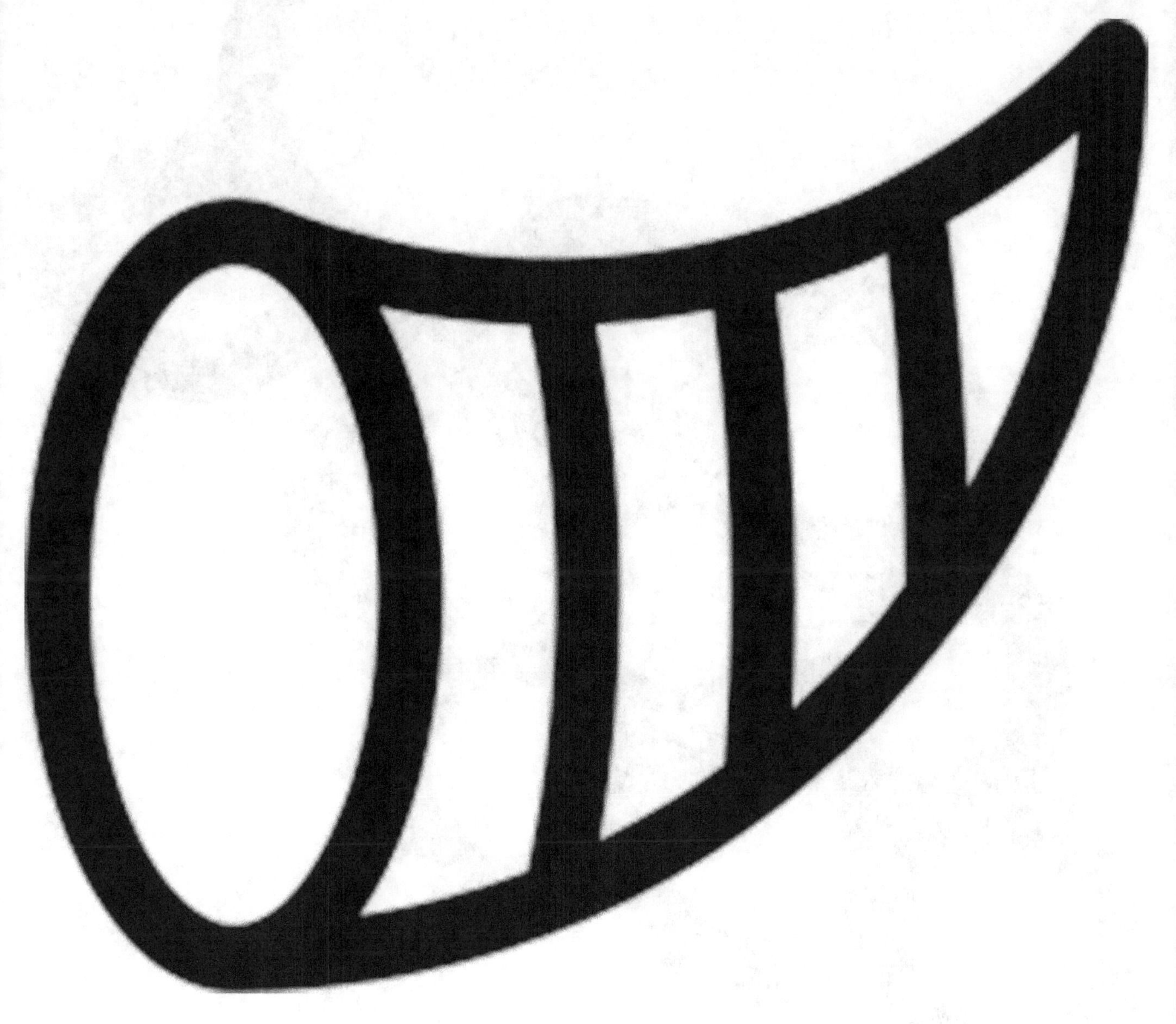

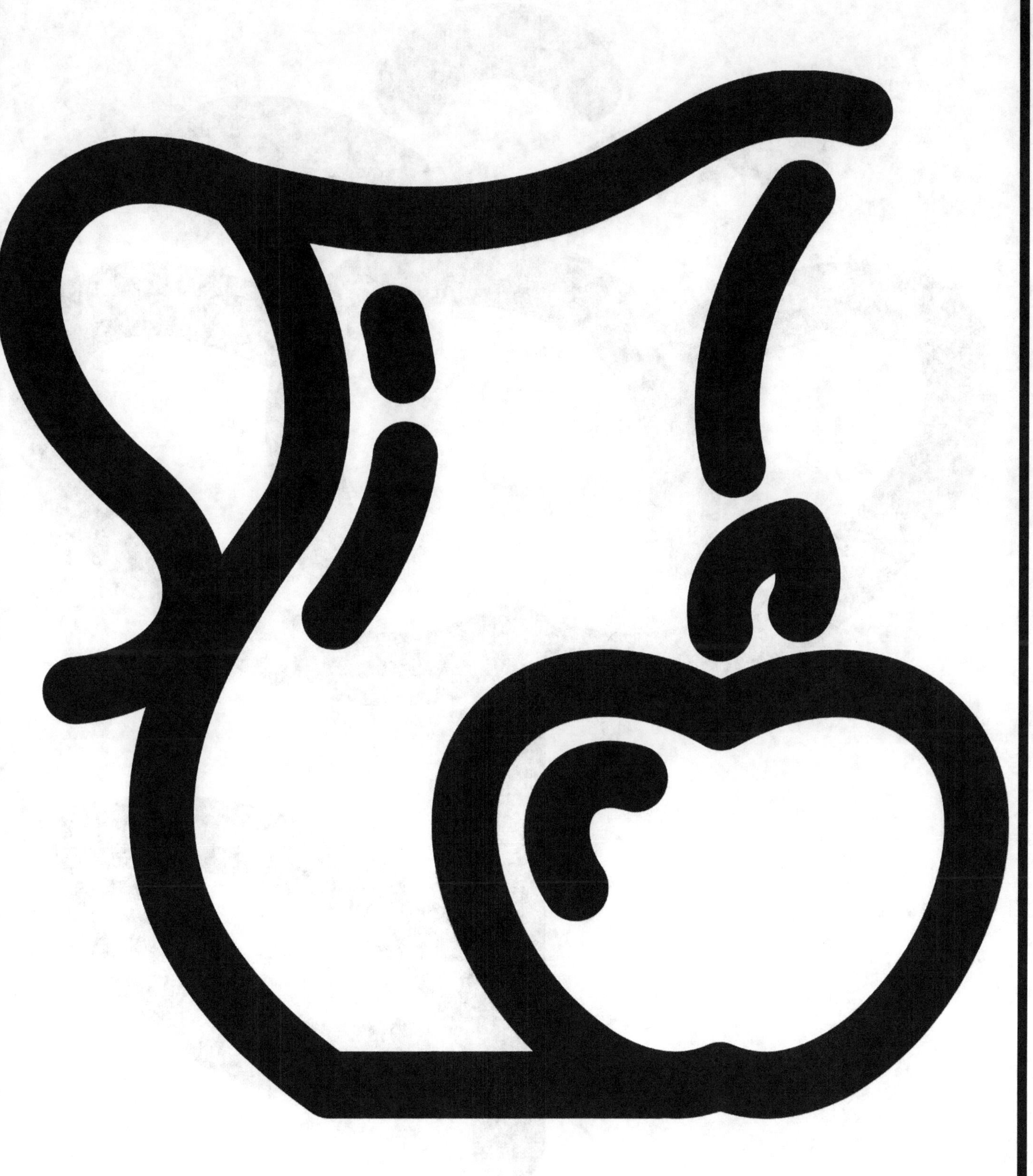

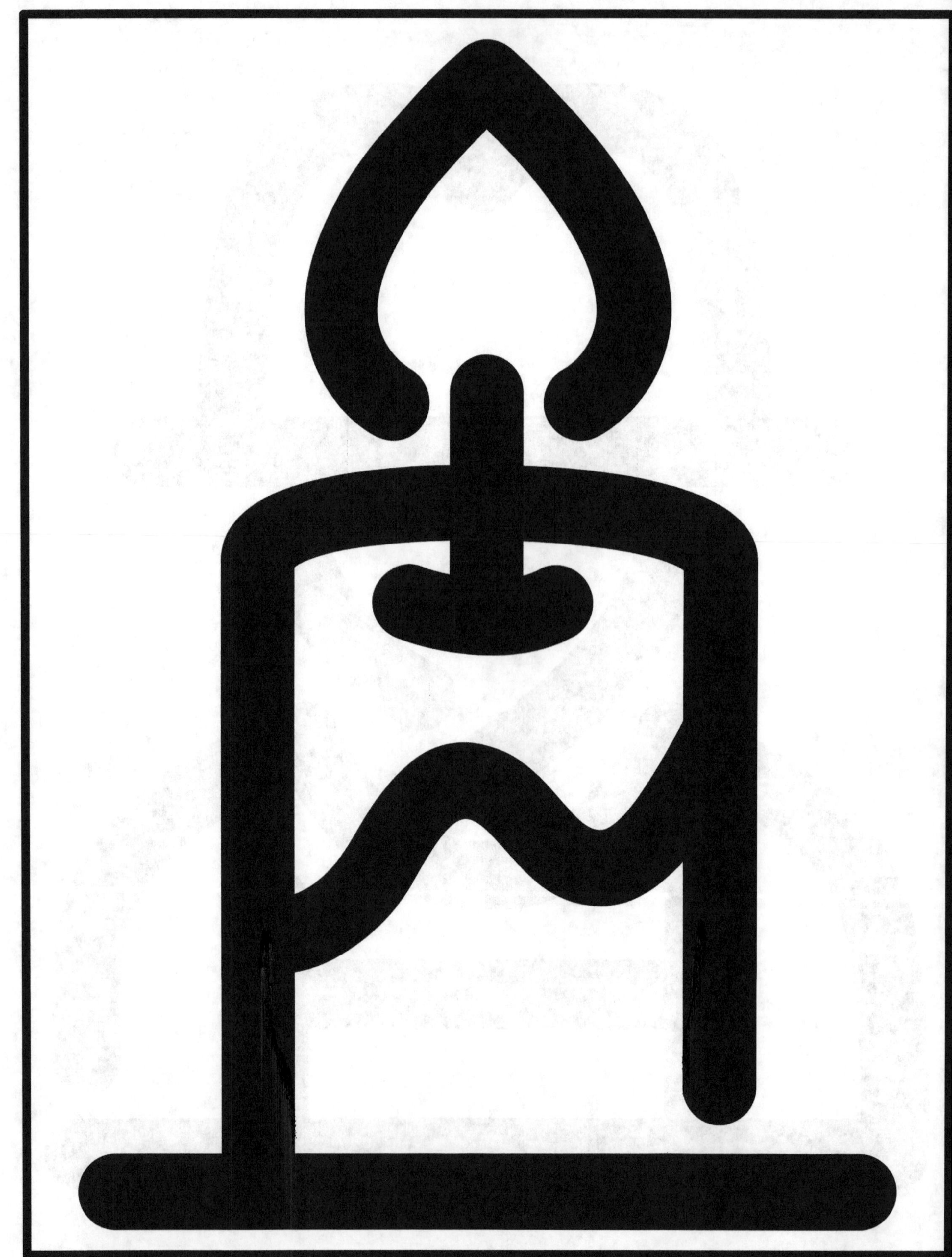

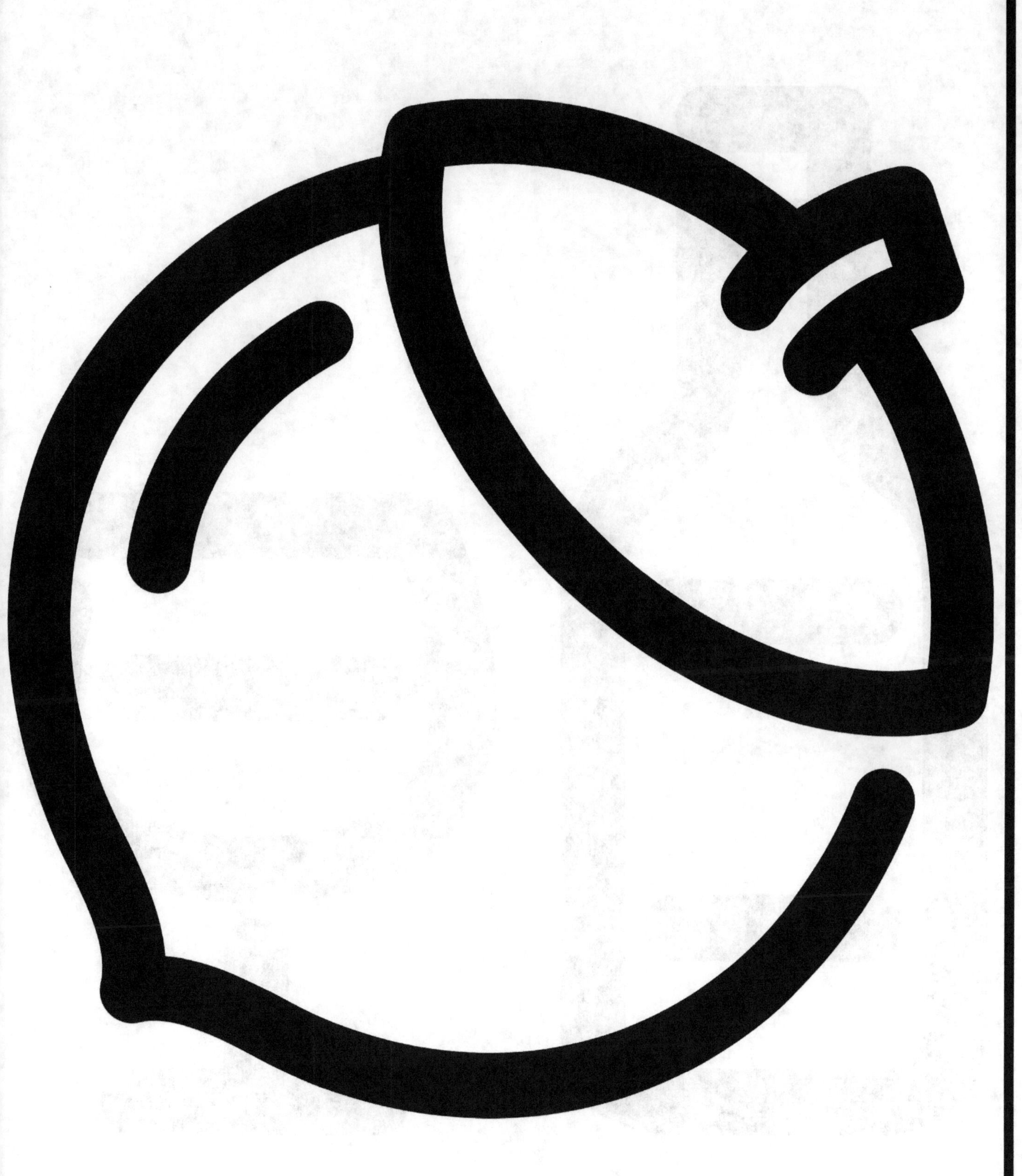

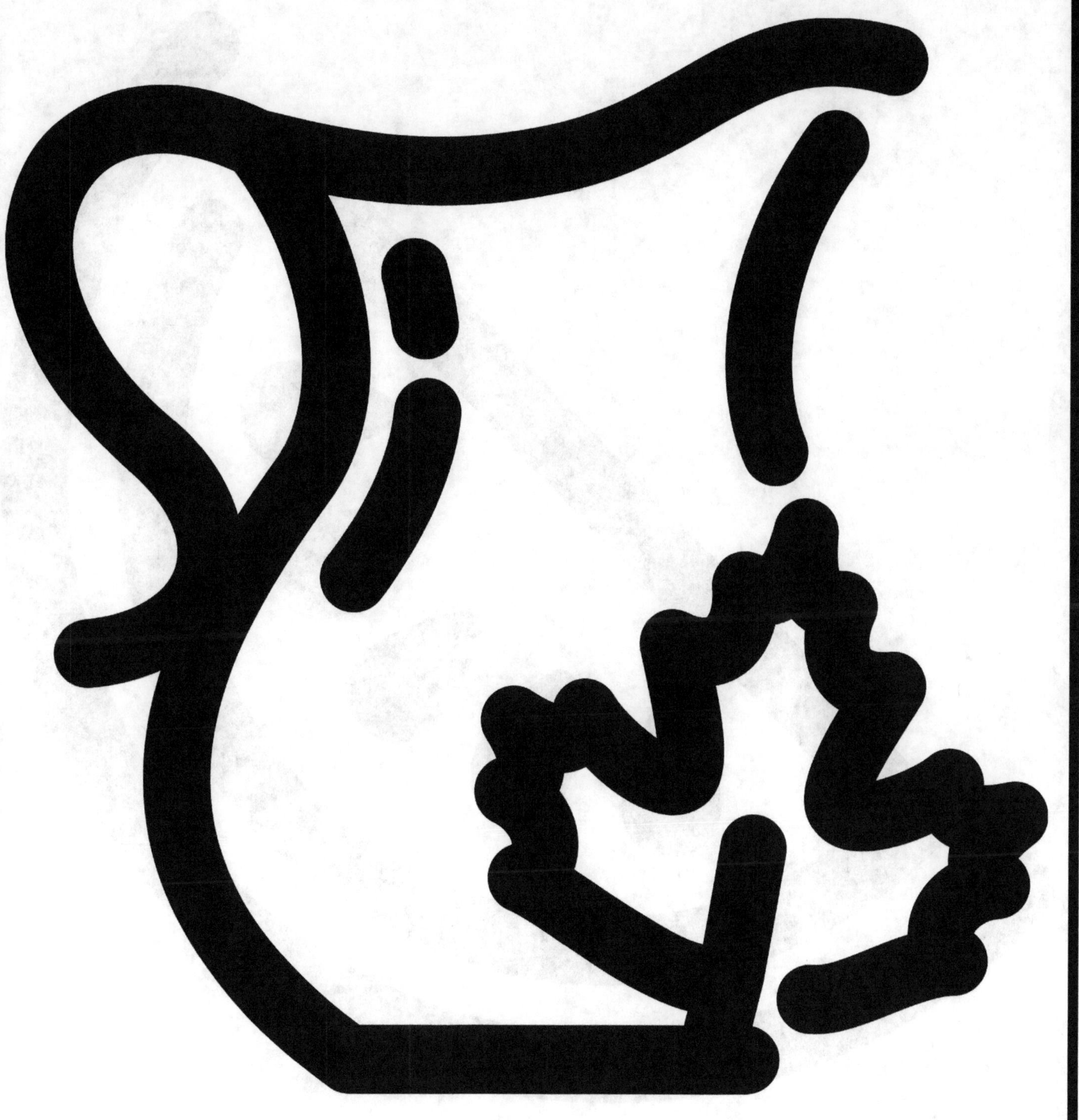

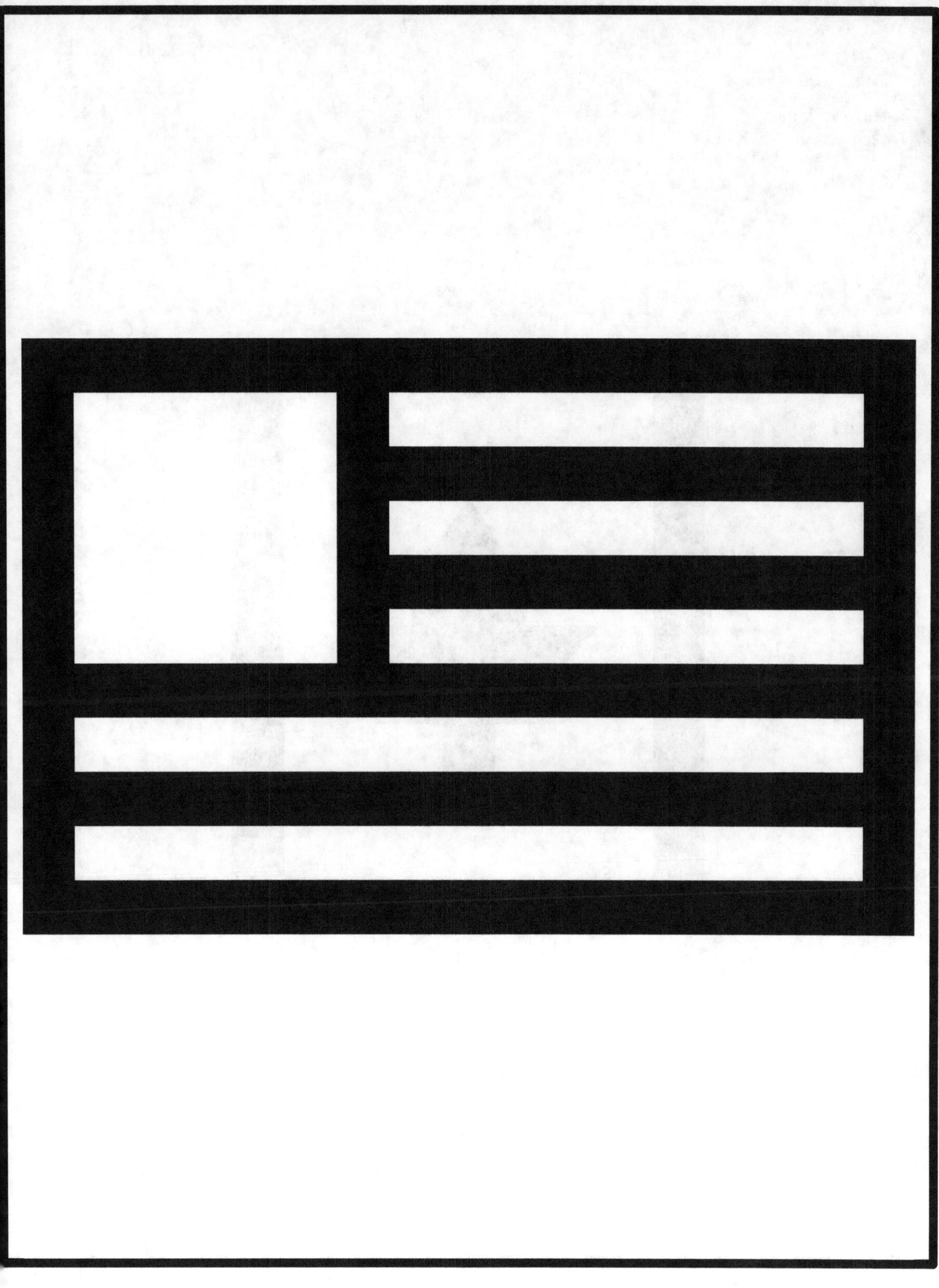

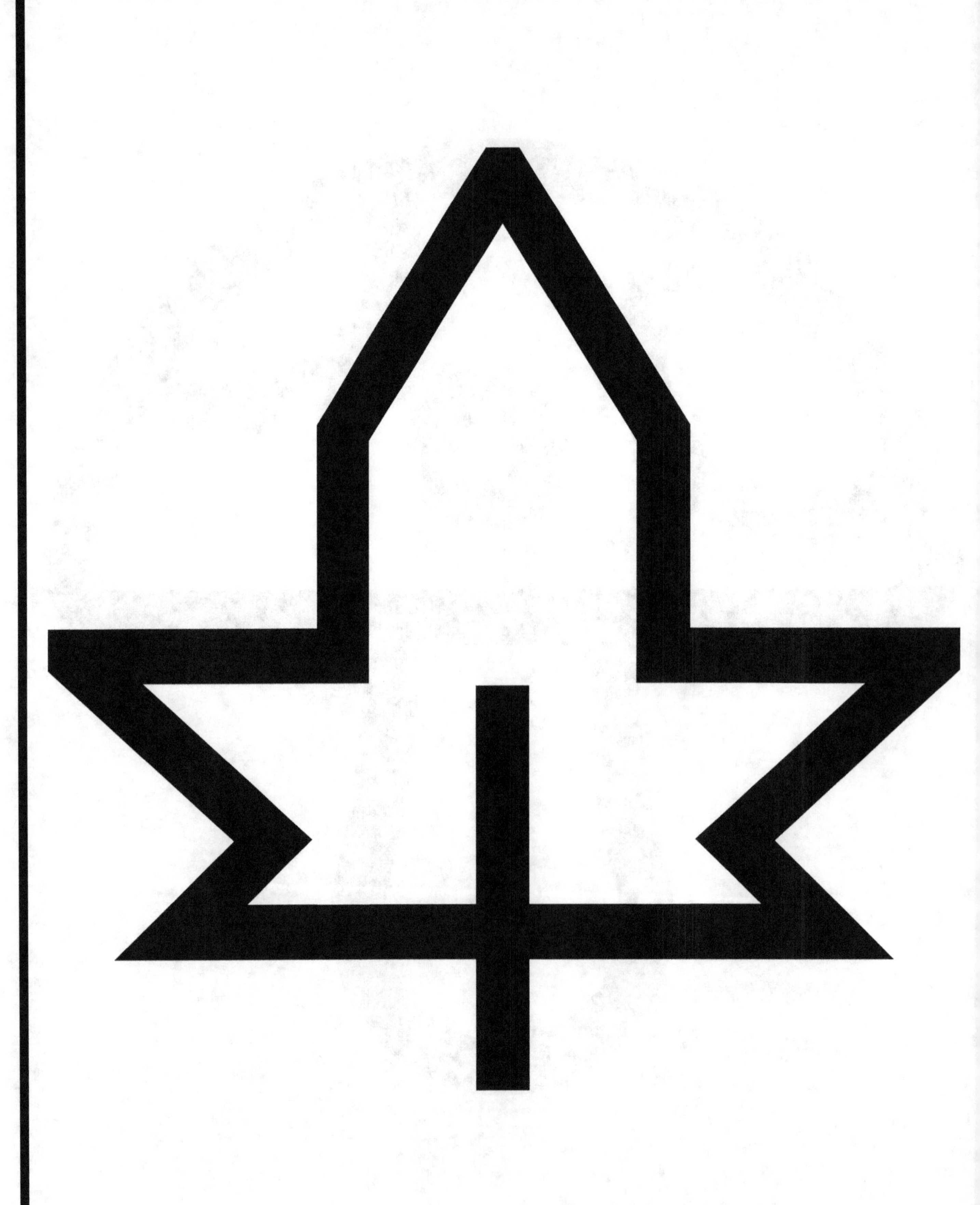

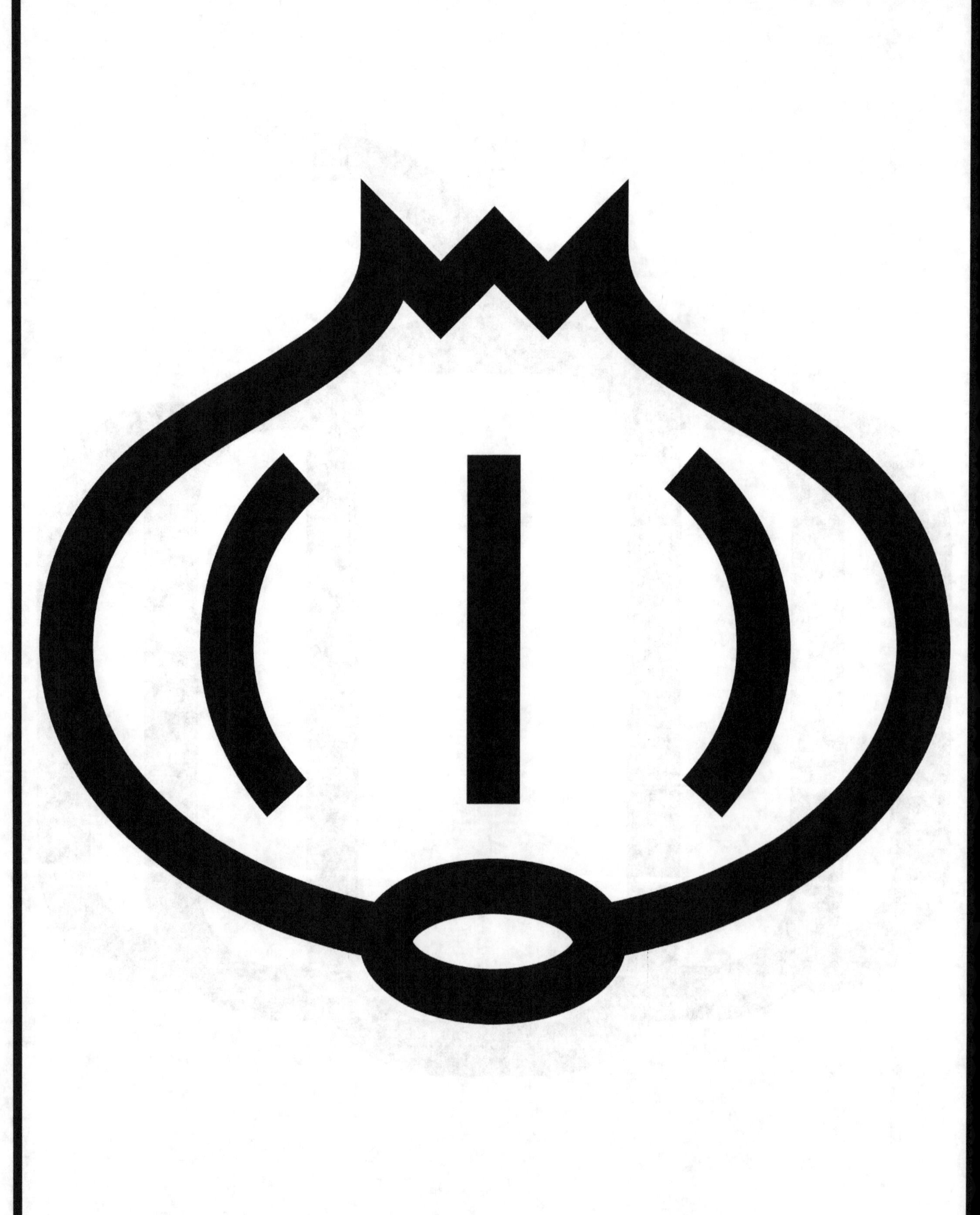

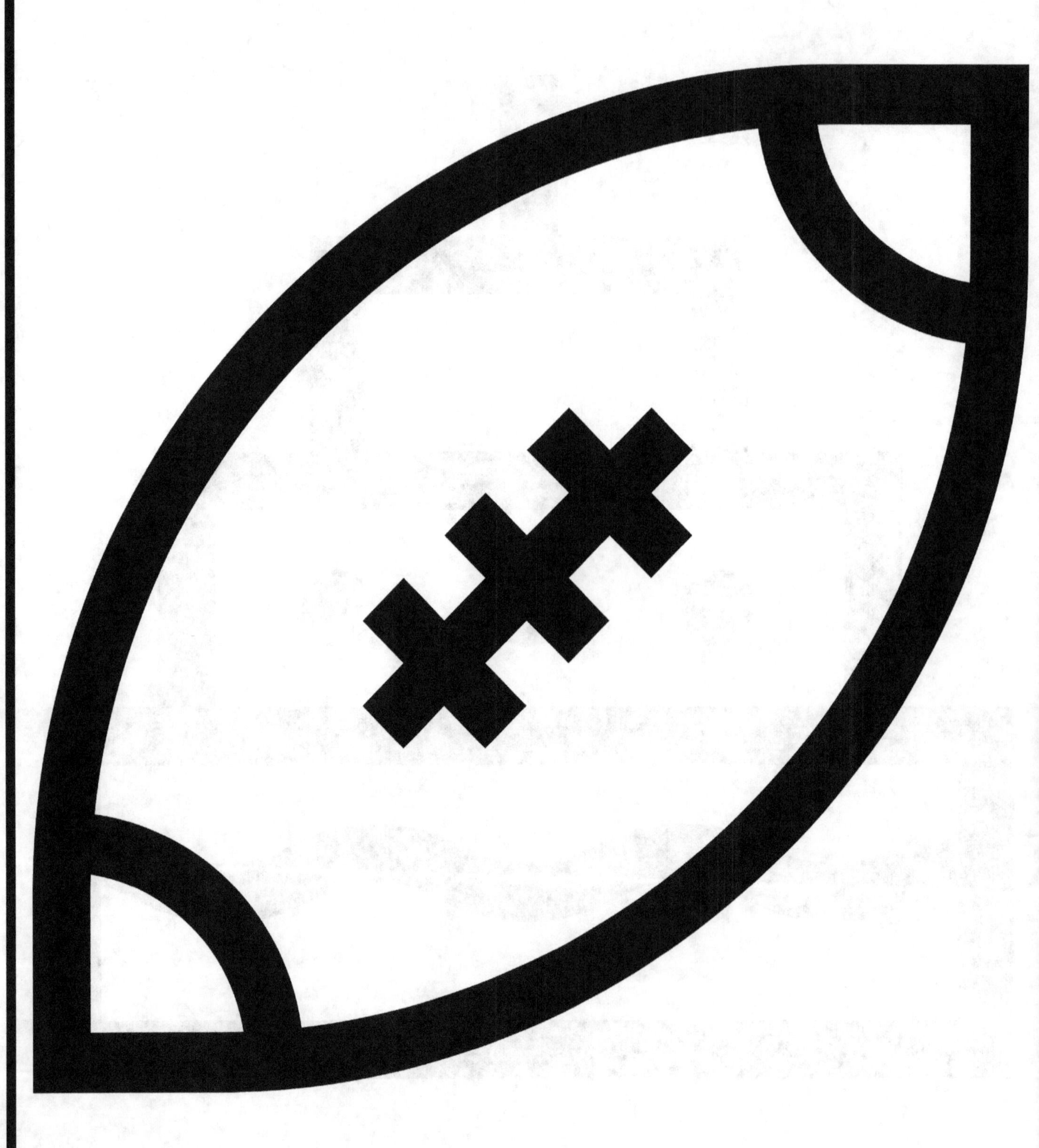

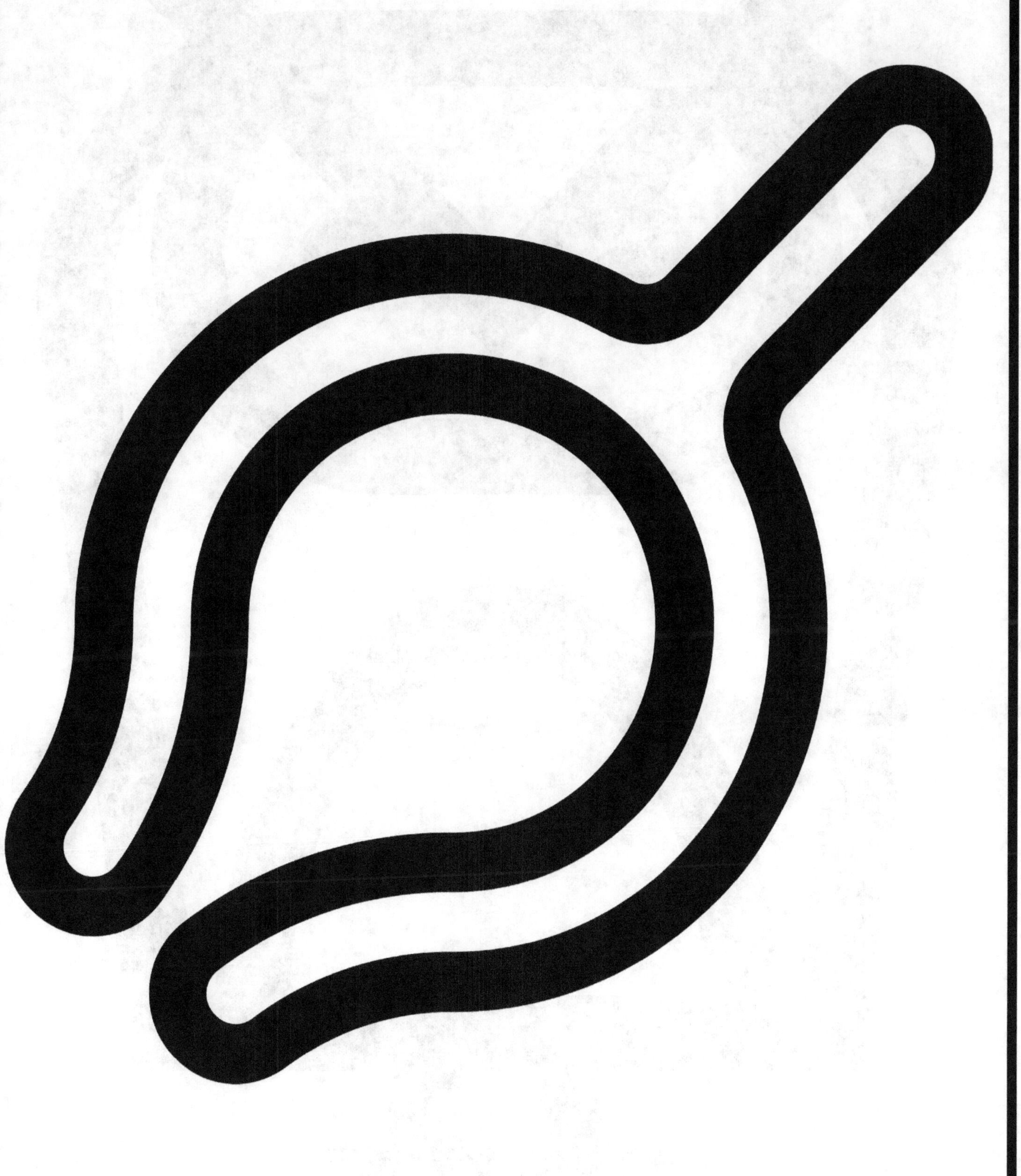

www.ingramcontent.com/pod-product-compliance
Lightning Source LLC
Chambersburg PA
CBHW081624250726

48657CB00009B/2709